Learn Meteor - Node.js and MongoDB JavaScript platform

Be ready for coding away next week using Meteor

Arnaud Weil

Learn Meteor - Node.js and MongoDB JavaScript platform

Be ready for coding away next week using Meteor

Arnaud Weil

ISBN 978-1-365-29120-3

© 2016 Arnaud Weil

To my wonderful family. Your love and support fueled this book.

To my Verallia and Bruitparif clients, whose demanding projects helped me discover and challenge Meteor.

Contents

1. **Introduction** 1
   1.1 What this book is not 1
   1.2 Prerequisites 1
   1.3 How to read this book 2
   1.4 Tools you need 2
   1.5 Source code 2

2. **Why Meteor ?** 3
   2.1 How I felt in love with Meteor 3
   2.2 Why is Meteor so productive? 4
   2.3 Where is the catch? 5

3. **Beginning with Meteor** 7
   3.1 Setting up your development machine 7
   3.2 Creating a meteor application 7
   3.3 What are those files ? 10
   3.4 Meteor is listening to your code 11
   3.5 The HTML file 11
   3.6 It's your turn to code: do-it-yourself 16
   3.7 Exercise - Create the application 17
   3.8 Exercise solution 17

CONTENTS

4. Blaze, Spacebars and reactivity **19**
    4.1   Spacebars 19
    4.2   Where does the data come from? 20
    4.3   Helpers 20
    4.4   Client and server code 22
    4.5   Organizing things 24
    4.6   Exercise - Display the current time 25
    4.7   Exercise solution 26
    4.8   Reactivity 28
    4.9   Available blocks 32
    4.10 Template events 37
    4.11 Data context 42

5. Managing data from a MongoDB database . . **45**
    5.1   What is MongoDB? 45
    5.2   Collections 46
    5.3   Exercise - Manually create a news collection in MongoDB 47
    5.4   Exercise solution 48
    5.5   Mongo.Collection 49
    5.6   Exercise: Display the news 54
    5.7   Exercise solution 55
    5.8   Query selectors 57
    5.9   Updating data with a Mongo.Collection . 59
    5.10 Exercise: Enable adding a piece of news . 61
    5.11 Exercise solution 62
    5.12 Exercise: Enable users to delete news . . 65
    5.13 Exercise solution 66

6. Packages: admin dashboard, navigation, validation, forms generation **69**

    6.1   What are packages 69
    6.2   Searching for and installing packages . . 70
    6.3   Back-office management 73
    6.4   Exercise: Create back-office for data management 74
    6.5   Exercise solution 75
    6.6   Navigation 76
    6.7   Exercise: Enable routing and create a layout 80
    6.8   Exercise solution 81
    6.9   Schemas, validation 83
    6.10 Exercise: Create a collection and schema for the products 86
    6.11 Exercise solution 87
    6.12 CRUD forms generation 88
    6.13 Exercise: Create GUI for the user to display and add products with validation . . 90
    6.14 Exercise solution 91
    6.15 Bootstrap 95
    6.16 Exercise: Add some style to the application 96
    6.17 Exercise solution 97

7. Accounts: user management **103**
    7.1   Meteor's account system 103
    7.2   Exercise: Secure the products management 107
    7.3   Exercise solution 108

8. Going further **111**
    8.1   MiniMongo: you don't even need MongoDB 111
    8.2   Exercise: Create and manage a shopping cart 113
    8.3   Exercise solution 114

CONTENTS

    8.4   Getting out of prototyping 120
    8.5   Exercise: Remove the *autopublish* package 125
    8.6   Exercise solution 125
    8.7   Exercise: Remove the *insecure* package . 129
    8.8   Exercise solution 129

Definitions **133**
    Bundling 133
    Minification 133
    npm 134
    Spacebars 134

A word from the author **135**

The Learn collection **137**

1. Introduction

1.1 What this book is not

I made my best to keep this book small, so that you can learn Meteor quickly without getting lost in petty details. If you're looking for a reference book where you'll find answers to all the questions you may have within the next 4 years of your Meteor practice, you'll find other heavy books for that.

My purpose is to swiftly provide you with the tools you need to code your first Meteor application and be able to look for more by yourself when needed. While some authors seems to pride themselves in having the thickest book, in this series I'm glad I achieved the thinnest possible book for my purpose. Though I tried my best to keep all of what seems necessary, based on my 14 years experience of teaching.

I assume that you know what Meteor is and when to use it. In case you don't, read the following *Why Meteor ?* chapter.

1.2 Prerequisites

In order for this book to meet its goals, you must :

- Have basic experience creating applications with JavaScript.
- Have working knowledge of HTML.
- Know what a Web application is.

1.3 How to read this book

This book's aim is to make you productive as quickly as possible. For this we'll use some theory, several demonstrations, plus exercises. Exercises appear like the following:

 Do it yourself: Time to grab your keyboard and code away to meet the given objectives.

1.4 Tools you need

The only tools you'll need to work through that book are:

- A Windows, Linux or OS X machine
- A text editor. My own favorite is the free Visual Studio Code[1], just pick the one you like

1.5 Source code

All of the source code for the demos and do-it-yourself solutions is available at https://bitbucket.org/epobb/learnmeteorexercises

---
[1] https://code.visualstudio.com

2. Why Meteor ?

If you're in a hurry, you can safely skip this chapter and head straight to the Beginning with Meteor chapter. This *Why Meteor* chapter is there for those that want to know why Meteor should be used.

2.1 How I felt in love with Meteor

I've been coding a lot of data-centric applications using various technology stacks. They usually involve displaying and updating data from some store (mainly a database) through a user interface and APIs, adding some functional logic in the way.

Problem is: most technology stacks involve writing quite some code for basic things, and often require different coding logics on the client and server.

One of my clients presented me with a challenging application to build. After rough evaluation of the time needed, writing a proof of concept required dozens of days. That was too much, so I took a full day and looked for available technology stacks. By the end of the day I stumbled upon Meteor. It promised a lot, but would it hold to its promises?

Well, it did. In five days I had the proof-of-concept coded and deployed on a staging server. A few days later it appeared that Meteor could also meet the requirements for another client's project, except that the requirements needed low-level network I/O. Turns out Meteor allowed me to leverage Node.js in a breeze, and I had the first draft running in hours.

I love tools that make me productive for common tasks while also allowing for greater power and customization when needed. Meteor does just that, providing simple ways to answer most requirements of today's applications.

2.2 Why is Meteor so productive?

Meteor makes writing applications a much faster process than many other Javascript environments. Here are some of the reasons why:

- Everything a developer needs is installed in a breeze, on any major OS (Linux, Windows, OS X);
- JavaScript code on the server and client, some of the code may even be shared between the two;
- Native support for MongoDB collections (if you don't know MongoDB we'll talk about it a bit later);
- Automated synchronization of the data between client and server;
- Very little code to write;
- Most of the functionality a developer usually needs is provided as easy-to-install packages;
- A very helpful command-line utility.

- Out-of-the-box effortless minification and file combine;
- Simple creation of packages;
- Integrated debugging of server code right in the browser;
- Straightforward unit-testing of created packages.

2.3 Where is the catch?

Too often you invest time and energy in a technology stack, only to find out its drawbacks a while later.

After some extensive use, Meteor drawbacks came when deploying. This is personal experience, but I was faced with two problems.

First, as long as you are willing to host your apps in Meteor's cloud solution (*Galaxy*), everything goes well. If you want to host Meteor apps in your custom environment, you'd better use a Linux machine. In which case things go quite smoothly when you don't require a server farm.

As of writing, deploying to a production Windows server was so difficult that I stopped in the process. That's a real pain, to say the less. This is strange since the Meteor team worked hard to bring excellent support for developing on a Windows environment. However, my problems were solved when using Docker for deployment. Dockerized Meteor applications can be deployed on any platform that support Docker, which means Linux, Windows or cloud with no surprise.

Second, the applications deployed had performance problems. There are many things that can be done in order to improve Meteor application performance, but it's quite a disappointment to spend a lot of time on performance improvements when the development stage was so quick.

All in all, though you can learn Meteor very quickly (that's the purpose of this book), bear in mind that fully understanding Meteor takes time. It's a quick way to create applications thanks to bold assertions from the Meteor stack and many things going on under the hood. You'll be able to create great Meteor applications within a few days, but you'll need to invest some time to fully understand Meteor's engine.

What I mean is that most tasks that usually take hours of coding will take minutes using Meteor, but during the first days be prepared to get stuck several times on some documentation reading. All in all you should gain a lot of time anyway, but you'll need to invest yourself in order to really master the Meteor stack.

3. Beginning with Meteor

3.1 Setting up your development machine

You can develop Meteor applications using a Windows, Linux or OS X machine, and this book applies to all of them.

In order to setup your machine, just point your browser to the install page[1].

For Windows machines, there is an installer. On a Linux or OS X machine, just type:

```
curl https://install.meteor.com/ | sh
```

3.2 Creating a meteor application

Meteor boosts your productivity as a developer. While most JavaScript development environments rely on the help of scaffolding tools like Yeoman in order to hide the fact that you need many files for even a basic application, Meteor needs only three files to code your application.

---

[1] https://www.meteor.com/install

You read well: three files. That's all there is to it. Of course you can use a full folder hierarchy and as many files as needed to organize your application, but that's optional. Simply put, Meteor applies a good coding pattern from the start: KISS (keep it simple).

Although you need only three files, Meteor even makes that process easy. Let me show you how I create my *demos* application. I'll use my demos to showcase the techniques I want you to learn, before you get some practice for yourself in the exercises. You'll soon create your own application, but for now please bear with me: sit and relax, and look at my demonstration.

I want my application to be called *demos* so I simply open a command line and type:

```
meteor create demos
cd demos
```

That's it! The first line creates a "demos" directory and adds three files to it. It also adds a `.meteor` folder, but it's just a local storage you won't need to manage or go into.

Time to run my application. Guess what? Yes, you're right: Meteor makes it simple. Again, using my command-line I type:

```
meteor
```

That's a shortcut for `meteor run`. It builds my application, runs a local MongoDB database server, and runs an HTTP server (using Node.js) that serves the application.

Now I can simply open a Web browser and type in the application URL:

`http://localhost:3000`

> In case you don't like the default port (3000), you can use the `--port` argument of the `meteor run` command.

What do I see in my browser? Well, not much but that's a good start:

Alright, I didn't code anything yet but I already have a local database and server that render an HTML page. Out of the box, that page doesn't do more than increase a counter when you click the button, but it won't take long to fill that page with data and functionality.

3.3 What are those files ?

As mentioned earlier, there are currently three files that make up my application. In fact, I could code my whole application using those three files. Of course, for maintenance purposes it would be a good idea to split them up, but that's fully optional.

Let's take a look at those files. We have:

- demos.html contains the HTML that renders on the client;
- demos.js contains code that executes on the server and/or the client, and may be used by the HTML code;
- demos.css is, well, the CSS that applies to your HTML;

Sounds obvious? Great! In fact it is, but we just overlooked a time-saving feature of Meteor: you can mix server **and** client code in the same file. More about that later.

3.4 Meteor is listening to your code

Time for some magic: if I change whatever of those files, the result will automatically appear in my browser after a few seconds. If you never used a good development stack this may not feel so natural.

When I typed the `meteor` command in my command-line, it didn't just build the application and listen for HTTP queries. It also stays there listening for file changes. When a change is detected it builds the application again, and it also sends a message to the connected browsers so that they reload.

As a developer, this means all you have to do is change your files, and your browser refreshes. Best of all, this also works in production: any connected browser to your application will automatically refresh with the latest version whenever you publish a new version.

3.5 The HTML file

Let me open the `demos.html` file. Here's what we find inside:

```
<head>
  <title>demos</title>
</head>

<body>
  <h1>Welcome to Meteor!</h1>

  {{> hello}}
</body>

<template name="hello">
  <button>Click Me</button>
  <p>You've pressed the button {{counter}} times.</p>
</template>
```

You can see three base elements: head, body and template. Those are the only three elements that can be at the root of your HTML. The template element will be repeated, but any other HTML element should be inside one of those three elements.

Let's detail those three elements.

head

When Meteor runs your application, it does a lot of stuff for you, including referencing the JavaScript and CSS file, plus bundling and minification for those. For this, it will locate the head element and add links to those generated resources there.

body

That's where you put the HTML that renders at first to the user. Sure, you may feel that this is the easiest place to put your HTML elements, but that would make maintenance a nightmare.

Since you're a clean developer (I know it, because you're still reading), you won't want to put more than a few lines inside the `body` element. Later, we'll mostly use it as display for our routing engine. But hey, we don't necessarily need a routing engine to be clean. So what I recommend you do here is only use references to your templates.

Did I say *templates*. Time to look at the third element.

template

As I said, this element will be repeated. You create as many templates as you want, provided you assign a different `name` attribute to each.

Then you reference your template elements from the `body` element or from other templates using the mustache syntax with a > element:

```
{{> templateName}}
```

> Alright, this is not pure HTML, we added some *mustache* syntax. More about this a bit later. Just accept it like that, for now.

body + template + template + ...

In fact, if we look again at the `demos.html` file, we can see such a reference:

```
<body>
  ...
  {{> hello}}
</body>

<template name="hello">
  ...
</template>
```

What this means is that the content of the `template` element named *hello* must go inside the `body` element.

Which means I can write:

```
<body>
  {{> header}}
  {{> someGreatInfo}}
  {{> footer}}
</body>

<template name="header">
  ...
</template>

<template name="someGreatInfo">
  ...
</template>

<template name="footer">
  ...
</template>
```

I could also reference a template from within another template:

```
<body>
  {{> home}}
</body>

<template name="home">
  {{> latestNews}}
  ...
</template>

<template name="latestNews">
```

```
    ...
</template>
```

Sure, I could elaborate on that syntax but I'll do that later. For now, you already learned a bunch of new things and it's time to put them into practice.

3.6 It's your turn to code: do-it-yourself

Now is your turn to grab the keyboard and code away. Oh, just let me explain you how that works, in case you're not familiar with my *Learn* books.

About exercises in this book

All of the exercises are linked together: you're going to build a small e-commerce application. You'll allow users to browse for your products, add them to their basket, and you'll also create a full back-end where the site administrators will be able to list, create, modify, and delete products.

In case you get stuck

You should be able to solve the exercise all by yourself. If you get stuck or don't have a computer at hand (or you don't have the prerequisites for that book, which is fine with me!), here's the solution. I'll provide the solution for all of the exercises in this book, right after each of them.

3.7 Exercise - Create the application

 Create a new Meteor application named *meteorshop*. Add a <h1> title to the page that reads "Shop in a hurry". Remove the button and counter.

Your application should look like the following:

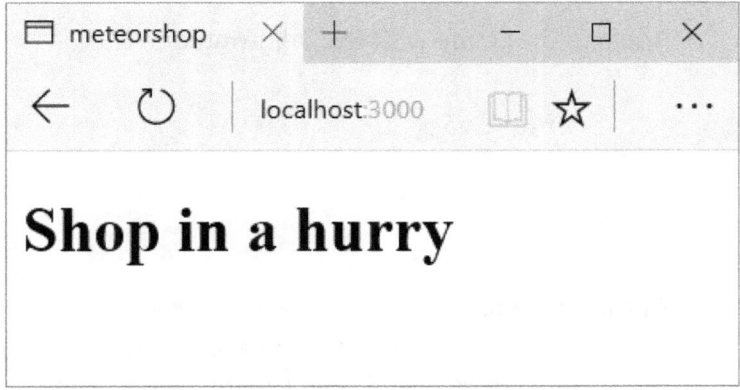

I know, it's basic, but you need to learn some more things before you can do more. Beginner badge unlocked: let's proceed to the next level.

3.8 Exercise solution

- Open a command-line and navigate to an empty development folder or create one.

- In the command-line, type `meteor create meteor-shop`.
- In the command-line, type `cd meteorshop`.
- Open the `meteorshop.html` file. Locate the following code:

```
<body>
    ...
</body>
```

- Replace that code with the following one :

```
<body>
    <h1>Shop in a hurry</h1>
</body>
```

- In the command-line, type `meteor`.
- Wait for the application to generate and run.
- Open your browser and type the following URL:

  http://localhost:3000

4. Blaze, Spacebars and reactivity

4.1 Spacebars

The mustache, or double brace syntax `{{ ... }}` is due to the fact that Meteor uses Spacebars as a view engine.

What if I prefer Angular or React?

Using Spacebars is no obligation and you can use another view engine. There are Meteor packages that allow you to use Angular, Angular2, React or Knockout.

This book will stick to the default Spacebars syntax since we get it out of the box.

Spacebars basics

As you saw, Spacebars is HTML on steroids. There are three main types of Spacebars blocks you can insert:

- `{{someValue}}` will evaluate `someValue` and render its content as text. More about that later;
- `{{> templateName}}` will insert a template named `templateName`, just like we saw above;

- `{{#block}}Your HTML content{{/block}}` will insert a template named `block` and provide the inner HTML to that template. There are built-in block templates that we'll see later like `if` or `each`.

4.2 Where does the data come from?

Once inside Spacebars' mustaches, you'll often need data. Consider the following code:

```
<div>You have {{messagesCount}} messages.</div>
{{#if hasMessages}}
   {{> messagesList data=messages}}
{{/if}}
```

In that code, we reference three values: `messagesCount`, `hasMessages` and `messages`. You must provide those values. Spacebars will look for it in the current context (more about this later), and then as helpers. Let's look at helpers.

4.3 Helpers

In the JavaScript file, I can add helpers that provide data for the view. That is, data that can be accessed from the Spacebars syntax in my HTML file.

In order to provide a value, we simply use the following syntax:

```
Template.templateName.helpers({
  someValue: function() {
    return ...;
  },
  someOtherValue: function(param1, param2) {
    return ...;
  },
});
```

Those helpers are readily available in my HTML file, so I could write:

```
<div>Here's a value: {{someValue}},
and another one: {{someOtherValue 'first param' 'seco\
nd one'}}</div>
```

Now let's look again at my previous example, this time writing the helpers.

demos.js

```
Template.messagesDisplay.helpers({
  messagesCount: function() {
    return 2;
  },
  hasMessages: function() {
    return true;
  },
  messages: function(param1, param2) {
    return ['Hello', 'Important message'];
  },
});
```

demos.html

```
<template name="messagesDisplay">
  <div>You have {{messagesCount}} messages.</div>
  {{#if hasMessages}}
    {{> messagesList data=messages}}
  {{/if}}
</template>
<template name="messagesList">
  <div>This one needs to be coded...</div>
</template>
```

4.4 Client and server code

What you write in the JavaScript files will be executed both on the client and the server. That can be very practical: much of the Meteor productivity comes from the fact that we can share the code that describes data and its shape in a single place and have it executed both on the client and server.

But sometimes your JavaScript code should be executed only on the server or the client. For instance, my templates need to be defined on the client only. There are two ways to achieve this.

Execute on server or client - testing in JavaScript

You can test the value of `Meteor.isClient` or `Meteor.isServer`, which return boolean values.

Here, I make sure my templates are defined only on the client:

demos.js

```
if(Meteor.isClient) {
  Template.messagesDisplay.helpers({
    ...
  });
}
```

Execute on server or client - using folders

You can create `client` and `server` folders inside your application, and Meteor will automatically ensure those files are processed only on the corresponding side.

For instance, here's a second way to ensure my templates are defined only on the client (note the file name):

client/demos.js

```
Template.messagesDisplay.helpers({
  ...
});
```

Still, if you want to write code that is executed on both the client and server, you can place your JavaScript file in the root folder or one that is not named `client` or `server`.

Which way would you prefer? It obviously depends on your project's size. You may want to have a single JavaScript file in a small project, hence use a test for `Meteor.isClient`. On a bigger project, you'll make maintenance easier if you place the files in the `client` and `server` folders.

Another advantage of using folders is that when you change files just in the `client` folder, Meteor builds your application faster than if you change them in the main or `server` folder. So using folders also makes your code-review experience faster.

> Should your application be really large, you can create the `client` and `server` folders as sub-folders, and the same logic will apply. This means you can have folders at the root of your application named after the functionality they hold, and each of those main folders would have `client` and `server` sub-folders when necessary.

4.5 Organizing things

In fact, you can use as little or as many files as you want. Meteor will look for all of the `template` elements in all of your HTML and CSS files, whether in the base folder, `client` sub-folder (or sub-sub-folder).

The same goes for the JavaScript file: Meteor will merge all of your JavaScript. The only detail, as we saw, is that JavaScript files located in the `client` folder will only execute on the client while those in the `server` folder will only execute on the server. Any other JavaScript file will execute both on the client and server.

4.6 Exercise - Display the current time

Time again for some fun: you're going to practice what we just saw.

Just like with the previous exercise, the solution follows, in case you need it. But I bet you won't.

 Add a new template named "timeDisplay", which displays the current time. Reference the `timeDisplay` template from the *body* element.

Your application should look like the following:

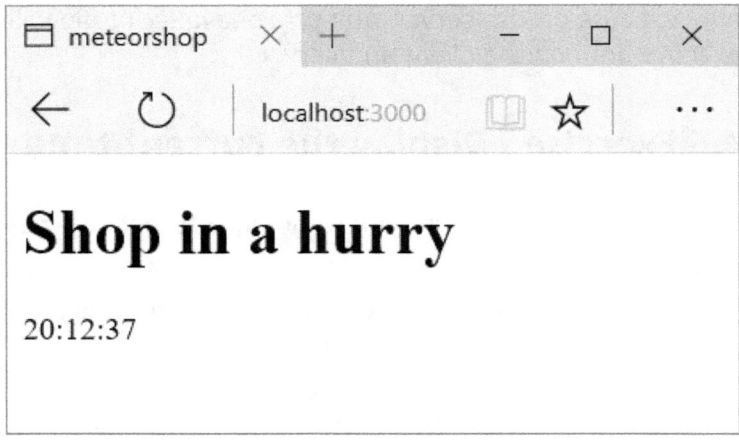

4.7 Exercise solution

- Leave your browser open and the `meteor` command-line running.
- Open the `meteorshop.html` file. At the end of the file, add the following code:

meteorshop.html

```
<template name="timeDisplay">
  {{currentTime}}
</template>
```

- In the `meteorshop.html` file, locate the following code:

meteorshop.html

```
<body>
  <h1>Shop in a hurry</h1>
</body>
```

- Replace that code with the following one :

meteorshop.html

```
<body>
  <h1>Shop in a hurry</h1>
  {{> timeDisplay}}
</body>
```

- Create a folder named `client`. Add a `client.js` file into it.
- Open the `client/client.js` file. Add the following code:

client/client.js

```
Template.timeDisplay.helpers({
  currentTime: function() {
    var now = new Date();
    return now.toLocaleTimeString();
  }
});
```

- Switch back to your browser and look at the result: http://localhost:3000

4.8 Reactivity

An example

Now, I'm sure you're wondering: how about making the time refresh automatically? Indeed, that would be nice. Because the time that's displayed in our application is already outdated.

I have good news for you: Meteor handles this in a very elegant way, just like other productive framework: you update the values in your JavaScript, and the HTML refreshes automatically.

If you used other frameworks like Angular or Knockout you're used to that kind of magic that makes a programmer's life much easier. Meteor takes it a step further, because it can automatically refresh the HTML when something changes on the server. In fact, it can even refresh the HTML when something changes in the database!

For now, we don't have any database and are coding on the client side. So it's not going to be impressive. But believe me, in a few paragraphs we'll use code that's even simpler in order to get data refreshing automatically all from the database down to the browser.

Let me open your `client/client.js` file and replace the following code:

client/client.js

```
Template.timeDisplay.helpers({
  currentTime: function() {
    var now = new Date();
    return now.toLocaleTimeString();
  }
});
```

With the following code:

client/client.js

```
Meteor.setInterval(function() {
 var currentDate = new Date();
 Session.set('now',
  currentDate.toLocaleTimeString()
 );
}, 1000);

Template.timeDisplay.helpers({
 currentTime: function() {
  return Session.get('now');
 }
});
```

Let's save it. If I look at my browser again, I can see the time is refreshing. Again, you may not be very impressed with that, since we could do the same with even less lines of jQuery or plain JavaScript. That's because my example is too simple, that is, the result is too simple for Meteor to shine.

However, you can see a very interesting thing about our code already: the `currentTime` helper doesn't state that it has to refresh. All it does is get some value from a "Session" and return it. A whole different part of the code is updating that "Session" value on a periodic basis.

Session is a client-side storage

Session is a place where you can store key-value objects. It is global: stored on the client and available to the whole application.

In order to store a value you write:

```
var myObject = {
  A: 'my value',
  B: 5
}
Session.set('someKey', myObject);
```

And you retrieve the value at another place using that code (note the key, `'someKey'`, is the same as the one used to store the data):

```
var storedValue = Session.get('someKey');
console.log(storedValue.A); // prints 'my value'
```

Session is a reactive source

Code that reads a session value using `Session.get` will be reevaluated if the value changes. Well, there are some conditions for code to be reevaluated (it all depends on where it is called from), but code in a helper fills that condition. That's what Meteor calls reactivity.

In my example above, as soon as I write the new time value to the session, the `timeDisplay` helper is evaluated again and its value inserted in the HTML that states `{{timeDisplay}}`.

Reactivity will save us a lot of boilerplate code: as long as we use reactive data, we only need to update the data and the UI that relates to it updates.

There are way more reactive sources

Session is just one of the reactive sources. There are more reactive sources, here are some of them:

- ReactiveVar, which you can instantiate to store any value.
- Database queries, that we'll see a bit later, used to store data coming from the database.
- Meteor.user, that holds information about the current user.
- Meteor.status, that holds information about the client-server connection.

Meteor packages will provide you with other reactive sources.

4.9 Available blocks

As we saw, there are several built-in block templates in Spacebars, apart from the ones you can define yourself. Let's have a look at them.

if

That one will display an enclosed block only if a condition is truthy. Like in the following example:

```
<h1>Comments</h1>
{{#if comments}}
   <div>{{comments.length}} comments</div>
{{else}}
   <div>No comment yet.</div>
{{/if}}
```

Note that the `else` block is optional. And remember: it's all reactive. Helper variables you use from the Blaze HTML code are reactive. Which means that the `if` block will go visible or hidden at any time the `comments` value changes.

Also, there is a handy `unless` block. If works exactly as the `if` block, except that the block goes hidden when the condition is truthy - the exact opposite of a `if` block. We could rewrite the above sample like that:

```
<h1>Comments</h1>
{{#if comments}}
   <div>{{comments.length}} comments</div>
{{/if}}
{{#unless comments}}
   <div>No comment yet.</div>
{{/unless}}
```

each

An `each` block repeats its contents as many times as necessary. You provide it with some collection, and the enclosed block will be inserted as many times as there are elements.

There are two ways to use the each block: implicit or explicit. Consider the following examples:

Javascript for both examples

```
Template.commentsIndex.helpers({
  comments: function() {
    return [
      { title='Some comment', author='Jane' },
      { title='Another one', author='Ted' }
    ];
  }
});
```

We then have two ways to use it:

Implicit each

```
<h1>Comments</h1>
<ul>
{{#each comments}}
  <li>{{title}} - by {{author}}</li>
{{/each}}
</ul>
```

Explicit each

```
<h1>Comments</h1>
<ul>
{{#each comment in comments}}
  <li>{{comment.title}}
    - by {{comment.author}}</li>
{{/each}}
</ul>
```

Both ways yield the same result: two comments are displayed. The difference is that the first one changes the data context against which the inner block (`<li>` in that case) is evaluated.

When using the first approach, the data context of the inner block is the particular comment for which that block is duplicated. That's why we only state `title` inside the double mustache: since the data context is a comment, we mean the `title` property of the current comment object. Inside the inner block, I cannot reference the `comments` object anymore, since it was in my parent context.

On contrary, when using the second approach the data context of the inner block remains the same as the parent data context. Only the `comment` variable contains the current comment.

On a first approach, the implicit syntax is tempting because it looks more simple. The problem is that you loose the ability to refer to the parent context from your inner block, which for real-life scenarios will often be limiting.

Consider a change to the above samples:

Implicit each - doesn't work

```
<h1>Comments</h1>
<ul>
{{#each comments}}
    <li>{{title}} - by {{author}}
        (out of comments.length comments)</li>
{{/each}}
</ul>
```

Explicit each - correct

```
<h1>Comments</h1>
<ul>
{{#each comment in comments}}
    <li>{{comment.title}}
       - by {{comment.author}}
        (out of comments.length comments)</li>
{{/each}}
</ul>
```

This is not a real-life sample, since I want my samples to be simple. However, just try and generate a table with dynamic columns using two nested each statements and you'll be stuck if you choose the implicit syntax.

Which one do I recommend? I guess it's clear that except for trivial views, the explicit statement is more powerful, more maintainable, and even more readable.

Some more

There are other blocks and you can define your own blocks. For instance, a `let` block lets you define a new variable in your data context. As a developer you know that the most important tools are loops and conditional execution, which is what `each` and `if` blocks provide. Let's keep things simple: now we know the necessary blocks.

4.10 Template events

We are now able to display stuff, and display it in a reactive way. Which means our users will always see up-to-date information. Now, wouldn't it be nice if they could interact with that information? Alright, it's not just nice, it's necessary: if we can't get users to act on their data, we might as well look for another job now.

For user interaction, we can write event handlers just like we wrote helpers. Helpers are for displaying information, events are for user interaction. Let's suppose I want to display a message to the user and change it whenever the user clicks a button. Here's the HTML (well, Blaze HTML):

client/timeDisplay.html

```
<template name="messageDisplay">
  <p>Message: {{sessionMessage}}</p>
  <button>Be nice</button>
</template>
```

My message will be stored as a session variable so that it is reactive. Here's the helper that returns the session value:

client/timeDisplay.js

```
Template.messageDisplay.helpers({
  sessionMessage: function() {
    return Session.get('message');
  }
});
```

Now, I want the message to change whenever the user clicks the button. So I simply add an event handler for that:

client/timeDisplay.js

```
Template.messageDisplay.helpers({
  ...
});

Template.messageDisplay.events({
  'click': function () {
    Session.set('message', 'Hello!');
  }
});
```

This event handler tells Meteor that whenever a `click` event is raised from the `messageDisplay` template, the code inside the function should be executed. The code I wrote changes a session variable, so the `sessionMessage` helper that relies on that session variable is evaluated again an the HTML is updated.

This is what the user sees in their browser:

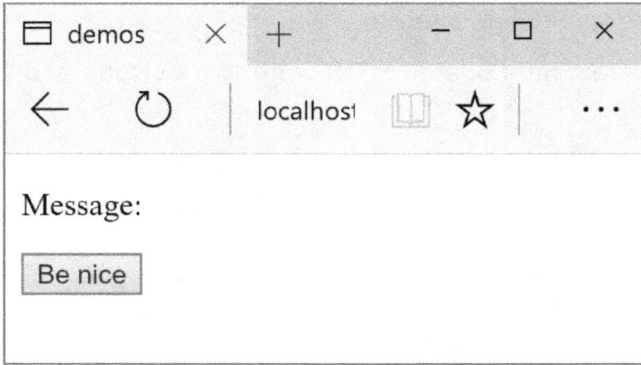

And this is what they see after clicking the button:

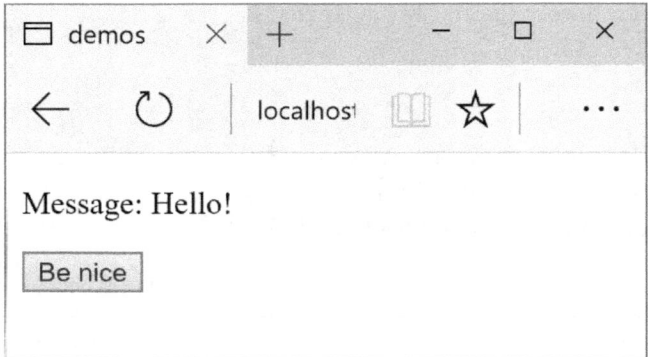

Now, how about adding a second button? If I do so, both buttons will raise the `click` event so I need a way to differentiate them. Fortunately, event handlers accept a CSS selector. So I can add an `id` or `class` to my HTML elements and use it in the event handler selector. I personally prefer to use `class` since `id` cannot be repeated. And who knows: my template may be used several time in the same page later on.

So here's my updated HTML with two buttons and CSS classes:

client/timeDisplay.html

```
<template name="messageDisplay">
  <p>Message: {{sessionMessage}}</p>
  <button class="nice">Be nice</button>
  <button class="cute">Be cute</button>
</template>
```

And the updated event handlers:

client/timeDisplay.js

```
Template.messageDisplay.helpers({
  ...
});

Template.messageDisplay.events({
  'click .nice': function () {
    Session.set('message', 'Hello!');
  },
  'click .cute': function () {
    Session.set('message', 'I love you.');
  }
});
```

Now each button displays a different message.

Of course, you can add as many event handlers as you want to a template, differentiating them using the event name and CSS selectors. What's more, when you write an event handler, your function can receive the event as parameter. More information in the Meteor documentation[1].

4.11 Data context

When referring to a field in a Blaze syntax, it's looked for in the current data context and helpers, as stated earlier. For instance, the following code will look for a `title` field in the current data context:

```
<p>You are looking at {{title}}.</p>
```

The data context can be provided using several tools:

- *each* and *with* blocks that change the current data context;
- *each .. in* and *let* blocks that add a field to the current data context;
- template code (*onCreated*, *onRendered*), where you can add fields to the data context using the *this* field which refers to the current template instance.

---
[1] http://docs.meteor.com/api/templates.html#eventmaps

I need you, super-hero !

Thank you so much for reading this book. I do hope that it helps you understand and get confident with Meteor.

As a reader, you are kind of a super-hero: you gain the power to create Web applications using Meteor and make the Web a better place.

Guess what? You have another superpower: to rate this book on the site where you purchased it. You may feel it's nothing, but it is super important for auto-edited books like this one. Please, take some minutes of your precious time to rate this book.

As a way to thank you, I'd like to offer you my upcoming book. Just drop me an email at books@aweil.com with a link to your rating, and you'll get my next book for free, before it is even published. Plus all my gratitude.

5. Managing data from a MongoDB database

5.1 What is MongoDB?

We're going to code an application, right? Most applications need to store data on some server in a way that is persistent and may be shared across all the users. Meteor chose to include MongoDB for that purpose, and is reportedly working on including other database engines.

MongoDB is very popular as a *no-SQL* database engine. Among the reasons that make it so popular is the fact that it works with a document format that's very close to JSON.

By default, MongoDB will not force you to use any schema, so you can simply store and read your data as needed. Which is great for getting your application ready as fast as possible.

Sure, you'll probably need some schema that your data should respect. Don't worry: that part will be covered extensively (and easily) by Meteor, as you'll learn later in this book.

5.2 Collections

In a MongoDB database you define collections, which are much like tables in relational databases. Except that collections can contain objects with different structures, and that those objects may have object or array properties. If you want to feel like you are using a relational database, just make sure that each object in a given collection has similar properties.

Meteor provides seamless support for MongoDB which we're going to learn very soon. However, you can always access the MongoDB database directly, from your command-line.

In my command line, I can type the following:

```
meteor mongo
```

Now all of my commands go to the MongoDB Node.JS engine, so I can issue direct JavaScript commands in order to manage the database. For instance, let's add an object describing a book to a collection named books:

```
db.books.insert({
  title: 'Learn METEOR',
  bought: true
});
```

This statement creates the collection in case it doesn't exist, and adds the object to it.

> You might think it's unnecessary to learn how to issue direct commands to the MongoDB engine. More since we want to learn Meteor quickly. Bad guess. Indeed, we shouldn't normally have to issue those commands manually, but that's not time wasted: Meteor accepts (almost) the same commands in JavaScript, whether on the client side or server side. Which means we're not only learning MongoDB, but also Meteor. Did I tell you I love Meteor? Oh, yes.

How about writing a query statement in order to check that the book is now part of the MongoDB database (technically, that we added a document to the books collection). Here it is:

```
db.books.find({});
```

That statement returns all of the books that are part of the database. It's the MongoDB equivalent of a SQL SELECT.

5.3 Exercise - Manually create a news collection in MongoDB

Now is finally time for you to practice. I guess your fingers are itching to code, so please accept my excuses for so much theory. That's in part because you needed to have

48 Managing data from a MongoDB database

that background before going on with this exercise... and also because I love speaking about Meteor.

 Open a Meteor MongoDB prompt and create a collection named `news` that contains the following documents:

{ title: 'Site just opened!'})

{ title: 'Special offers today.'})

Query the `news` collection in order to ensure you did your job correctly. You should get the following display (with different ObjectID) values:

```
C:\Windows\system32\cmd.exe - meteor  mongo
meteor:PRIMARY> db.news.find({});
{ "_id" : ObjectId("56d72cdbded5ae0b6018e60f"), "title" : "Site just opened!" }
{ "_id" : ObjectId("56d72cdbded5ae0b6018e610"), "title" : "Special offers today." }
meteor:PRIMARY>
```

5.4 Exercise solution

- Leave your browser open and the `meteor` command-line running.
- Open a new command-line and browse to your application folder.
- Type the following command:

```
meteor mongo
```

- On the MongoDB command-line that appeared, type the following code:

```
db.news.insert({ title: 'Site just opened!'} );
db.news.insert({ title: 'Special offers today.'} );
```

- On the same command-line, type the following code:

```
db.news.find({});
```

- Ensure the two objects appear in the results that were displayed by this command.

5.5 Mongo.Collection

Now comes one of the greatest time savers in Meteor. When developing traditional client-server applications you have to write server code that accesses the data source, exposes it to the client (i.e. write an API), and consume that API from the client. You have to track changes on the client, submit them to the server (API again), and write server code that pushes those changes to the data source. Optionally, you would write code that detects changes in the data source and pushes them to the client.

Meteor takes an approach where it does all of that by default, as long as you create a `Mongo.Collection`. Which means little code to write and maintain, and more time to go on holiday, have fun with your kids or play that great MMORPG you like.

Basically, you create a `Mongo.Collection`, query it, and Meteor does what is needed for that to work. That means writing two lines:

```
Books = new Meteor.Collection('books');

var allBooks = Books.find({});
```

Practically, those two simple lines have several effects:

- Provide you with access to the collection on the server side.
- Create a MiniMongo database on the client side. MiniMongo holds the query results on the client side and provides (almost) the same interface as the MongoDB database.
- Ensure that the MiniMongo database is kept in sync with the server-side MongoDB database: any change to the query result will be pushed to the client for you.

With Meteor, the data management schema for that (and other) collection looks like this:

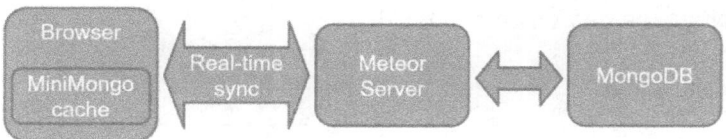

Remember I created a books collection in the Collections chapter? I'm going to display it in my application.

In order for the client and server to know about that collection, I just have to create a Meteor.Collection. In order to get the collection to be displayed in my templates, I'll add a helper. Here's the full JavaScript code:

demos.js

```
Books = new Meteor.Collection('books');

if (Meteor.isClient) {
  Template.books.helpers({
    books: function () {
      return Books.find({});
    }
  });
}
```

The first line is executed both on the client and server. It ensures that they both can access the books collection stored in the MongoDB database. Then, we create a template helper that exposes all of the books as a "books" variable in the context. Note that we use the find() method that MongoDB accepts, with the same syntax.

Now, we can write the HTML:

demos.html

```
<template name="books">
    <ul>
        {{#each book in books}}
        <li>{{book.title}}</li>
        {{/each}}
    </ul>
</template>
```

And here's the result:

Now comes the best part: this simple code is fully reactive all the way down from the server to the client. Which means I have nothing to do in order to get connected browsers to display any change in the books collection. Don't just take my word for it, let me demo it.

I'll pop open a command line and type:

```
meteor mongo

db.books.insert({
  title: 'Learn WebSockets',
  bought: false
});
```

Let's switch back to the browser. I don't even need to refresh it. Here's the display:

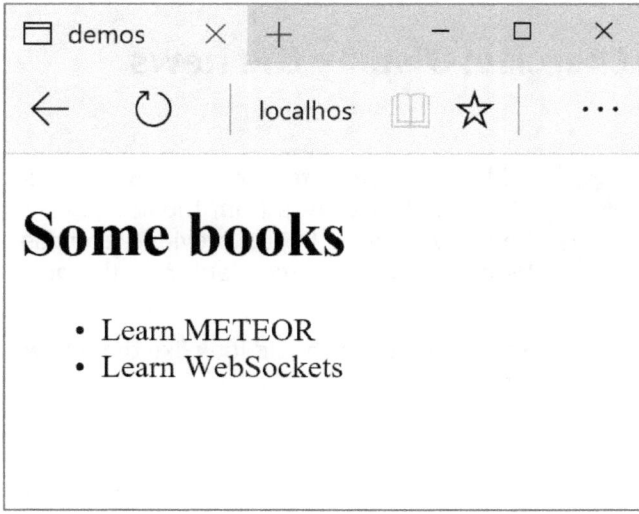

Yes, the inserted book appeared. Whenever we query a `Meteor.Collection`, Meteor ensures that the query results are synchronized real-time between the server and clients. It uses a WebSocket for that. Internally, Meteor's *DDP* protocol is used for changes to be pushed to the clients.

Those are really good news. I told you that Meteor makes us productive, and I hope it gets clearer to you as you read through that book. That is a really good example: using only basic code, we have no effort to make in order to get real-time synchronization between all connected clients. Just think for one second how easy it is to write real-time applications like chat or collaborative applications: a change on one client is reflected to the server and all connected clients. Nifty and effortless.

5.6 Exercise: Display the news

Add a new template named "news", which displays all the news from the `news` collection you created in the previous exercise. Reference the `news` template from the *body* element.

Your application should look like the following:

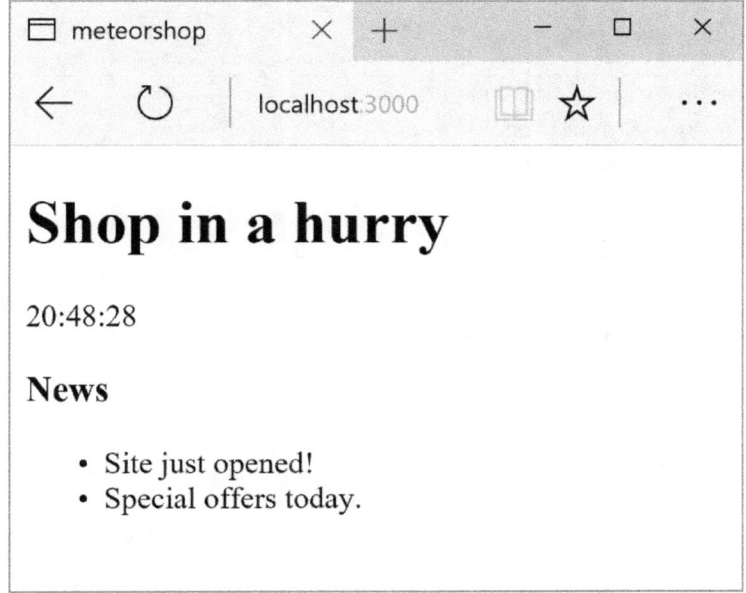

5.7 Exercise solution

- Leave your browser open and the `meteor` command-line running.
- Open the `meteorshop.js` file. Add the following code:

meteorshop.js
```
News = new Mongo.Collection('news');
```

- Open the `client/client.js` file. Add the following code:

client/client.js

```
Template.news.helpers({
    news: function () {
        return News.find();
    }
});
```

- Add a `news.html` file to the `client` folder. Add the following code:

client\news.html

```
<template name="news">
    <h3>News</h3>
    <ul>
        {{#each news}}
        <li>{{title}}</li>
        {{/each}}
    </ul>
</template>
```

- In the `meteorshop.html` file, locate the following code:

meteorshop.html

```
<body>
  <h1>Shop in a hurry</h1>
  {{> timeDisplay}}
</body>
```

- Replace that code with the following one :

meteorshop.html

```
<body>
  <h1>Shop in a hurry</h1>
  {{> timeDisplay}}
  {{> news}}
</body>
```

Switch back to your browser and make sure that the news are displayed.

5.8 Query selectors

In order to get the books in my example, I wrote the following statement:

```
Books.find({});
```

That is, I used the `find` method of the `Mongo.Collection` class. This command returns all of the documents in a collection. The first parameter is a query selector.

> Query selectors are used everywhere we need to reference some documents using MongoDB. They are roughly the equivalent of the WHERE part in a SQL statement. We'll use them later on when updating the data.

A selector is a JavaScript object. A default, empty selector is {}, which means all documents in the collection. Let's learn how to further refine our queries. Since we added title and bought fields to our Books collection, we can query using them.

Suppose we want to get only the books that were bought. We could use the following query:

```
Books.find({
  bought: true
});
```

And if we want those whose title is "Diet" and were not bought already, we can write:

```
Books.find({
  title: 'Diet',
  bought: false
});
```

As you may know, MongoDB being an unstructured database, we could use that selector even if some of the documents in the Books collection didn't have those fields.

How about finding all books that do not contain a `title` field and whose price is less that 10? Here you go:

```
Books.find({
  title: { $exists: false },
  price: { $lt: 10 }
});
```

You can find the whole query syntax reference in the MongoDB reference[1].

5.9 Updating data with a Mongo.Collection

The `Mongo.Collection` class offers update methods (almost) just like MongoDB. You surely remember that in order to add a book I connected directly to the database command-line interface and typed:

```
db.books.insert({
  title: 'Learn METEOR',
  bought: true
});
```

Now, thanks to Meteor I could write the following JavaScript code either on the client or the server:

---

[1] https://docs.mongodb.com/manual/reference/operator/query/

```
Books.insert({
  title: 'Learn METEOR',
  bought: true
});
```

When ran on the client it would in effect add the book to the client cache of the collection (which makes it instantaneous), then to the server collection inside MongoDB, then reflect any server change to the client, so that the client takes into account any change that could arise on the server.

The following methods are available (among others):

- `insert(document)` inserts a new document in the collection and returns its ID;
- `remove(selector)` removes all documents form a collection that match the provided selector;
- `update(selector, modifier)` updates all documents form a collection that match the provided selector, using the provided modifier.

For the `update` method, the modifier is a MongoDB modifier, or a document. A modifier contains '$' fields, while a document doesn't. If you provide a document, it completely replaces the existing documents. A modifier allows you to specify only some updates that need to be done to the matching documents.

Suppose I want to increase to 15 the price of all the books whose price is less than 10. I can write:

```
Books.update(
  { price: { $lt: 10 } },
  { $set: { price: 15 } }
);
```

> On the client side, there are limitations to which updates can be done using the *insert*, *update* and *remove* methods. They can be somewhat removed using the *allow* and *deny* methods of the *Mongo.Collection* class. You can learn more about that in the manual[a].
>
> [a]http://docs.meteor.com/api/collections.html#Mongo-Collection-allow

5.10 Exercise: Enable adding a piece of news

Inside the template named "news", add a new `input` element inside a `form` element. When the user types a text and presses enter, make sure that a new document is added to the `news` collection, with `title` fields that corresponds to the typed text.

Your application should look like the following:

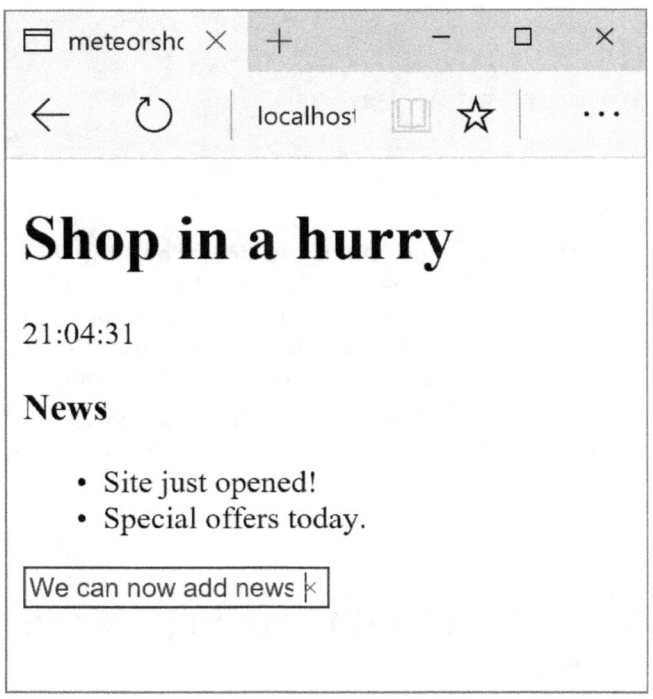

5.11 Exercise solution

- Leave your browser open and the meteor command-line running.
- In the `client/news.html` file, locate the following code:

client/news.html

```
<template name="news">
  <h3>News</h3>
  <ul>
    ...
  </ul>
</template>
```

- Replace that code with the following one :

client/news.html

```
<template name="news">
  <h3>News</h3>
  <ul>
    ...
  </ul>
  <form>
    <input type="text" name="title" placeholder="Titl\
e" />
  </form>
</template>
```

- Open the `client/client.js` file. Add the following code:

client/client.js

```
Template.news.events({
  'submit form': function (e) {
    e.preventDefault();
    var title = e.target.title.value;
    News.insert({title: title, created: new Date()});
  }
});
```

Switch back to your browser and make sure that you can add some piece of news by typing them in the newly created input field.

> ### Meteor magic
>
> As you already know, Meteor ensures that any change made on the server is pushed to any connected client. But don't take my word for it: you can now ensure it is true.
>
> Open two browser windows using the following URL:
>
> *http://localhost:3000*
>
> Add a piece of news in one of the windows, it should appear instantly in the other. Great, isn't it? And it would work exactly the same should you deploy that application to a distant server.

5.12 Exercise: Enable users to delete news

 Inside the template named "news", next to each piece of news add a button. When the user clicks that button, the corresponding piece of news should be deleted from the database.

Your application should look like the following:

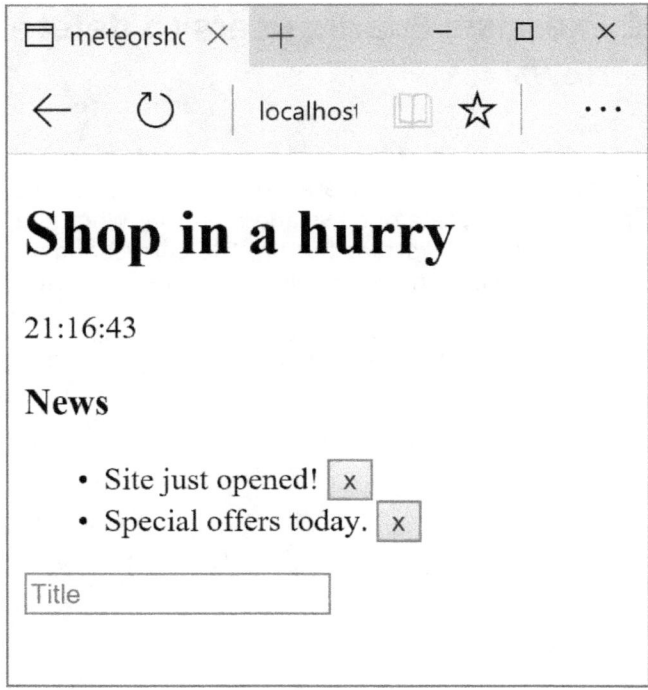

5.13 Exercise solution

- Leave your browser open and the `meteor` command-line running.
- In the `client/news.html` file, locate the following code:

client/news.html
```
<li>{{title}}</li>
```

- Replace that code with the following one :

client/news.html
```
<li>{{title}} <button class="removeAction">x</button>\
</li>
```

- The full news template should now be: :

client/news.html
```
<template name="news">
  <h3>News</h3>
  <ul>
    {{#each news}}
    <li>{{title}} <button class="removeAction">x</but\
ton></li>
    {{/each}}
  </ul>
  <form>
    <input type="text" name="title" placeholder="Titl\
e" />
  </form>
</template>
```

- Open the client/client.js file. Locate following code:

client/client.js

```
Template.news.events({
  'submit form': function (e) {
    ..
  }
});
```

- Replace it with the following code:

client/client.js

```
Template.news.events({
  'submit form': function (e) {
    ..
  },
  'click .removeAction': function(e, a) {
    News.remove({_id: this._id});
  }
});
```

Switch back to your browser and make sure that you can delete pieces of news by clicking the button on their right.

6. Packages: admin dashboard, navigation, validation, forms generation

6.1 What are packages

Up to now, we've been manually coding our application. Meteor makes this part fast and painless, but if you stop reading now you'll find yourself repeating the same kind of code in most of your applications.

Creating user interfaces for input, validating data, handling navigation, tracing and many other tasks are not specific to one particular application. Their code can be factored and reused into packages.

You may already know about the npm package manager famous in the JavaScript community. Meteor being about JavaScript, we can sure use npm and get access to its active and wide range of packages. Which is great, however Meteor has its own package manager which provides packages specifically written for Meteor. The advantage of Meteor-specific packages is that they know of and benefit from all the tools that make Meteor so productive:

Packages: admin dashboard, navigation, validation, forms generation

client synchronized database cache, isomorphic code, authentication, and lots of other Meteor assumptions.

Meteor's package manager is Atmosphere. It is made of a web site and integrated as part of the Meteor command line.

> Atmosphere is bound to be progressively abandoned in favor of npm. As the Meteor guide states[a]:
>
>> With the release of version 1.3, Meteor has full support for npm. In the future, there will be a time when all packages will be migrated to npm, but currently there are benefits to both systems.
>
> However, as of now, Atmosphere is a recommended tool since it is both easy-to-use and productive tool.
>
> ---
> [a] https://guide.meteor.com/atmosphere-vs-npm.html

6.2 Searching for and installing packages

Searching for a package is done using the Atmosphere web site[1]:

---
[1] https://atmospherejs.com/

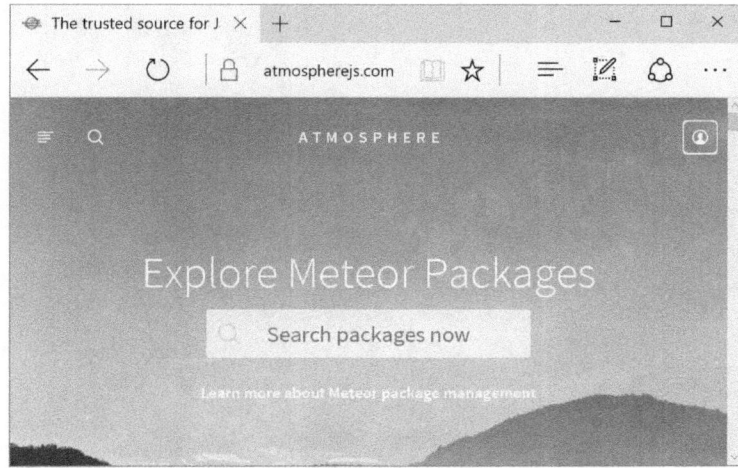

Suppose I need to create a REST API for CRUD operations on my collections. There are several packages for that. Hopefully Atmosphere shows the number of stars and installs for each package. Another useful information for selecting a package is the project activity (on the package page): when was it last updated, and is it updated on a regular basis? A quick search leads me to the *nimble:restivus* package:

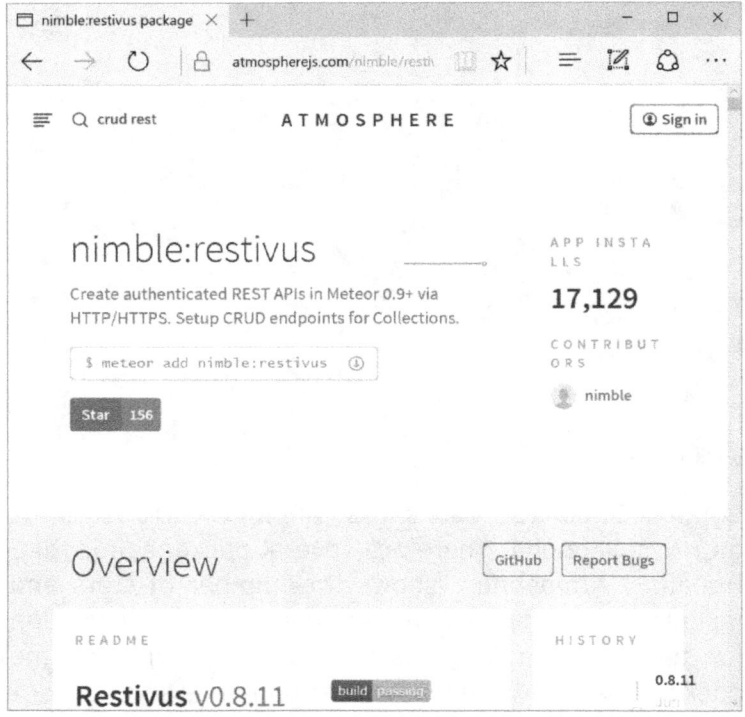

Once you find a package you simply add it through the command-line. For instance, if I want to use the *nimble:restivus* package I simply type the following command:

```
meteor add nimble:restivus
```

You can leave your meteor application running and open a new command line in order to type that command.

Just make sure the current directory is the one of your application.

It's time to have a look at some commonly used packages. That should help make you familiar with Meteor's packages productivity boost, and you'll soon find yourself searching through Atmosphere for an appropriate package once faced with a common task.

6.3 Back-office management

There will be several collections in our application. Though the end-user interface will allow for most common interactions with the collections, it would be nice to have a tool that allows for every CRUD operation through a nice GUI. Admin packages are made for this.

For instance, the *houston:admin* package provides us with a gorgeous admin GUI just by installing it. It hooks itself to the user management features of Meteor, which in turn allows us to hook it to practically any way of authenticating users, or use the default collection.

The *houston:admin* package requires no configuration, but it can be customized to better suit your needs when needed. Using it is a simple process:

1. **Add it typing** `meteor add houston:admin`
2. **Navigate to the** `http://localhost:3000/admin` **page**
3. **Create an account and give it admin rights**

Packages: admin dashboard, navigation, validation, forms generation

> If you use another account manager package or already created a user, you will simply be prompted for confirmation that you want to make the current user an admin.

6.4 Exercise: Create back-office for data management

Add the *houston:admin* package to your application. Create a user and give it admin rights so you can access the admin page. Make sure you can create, update and delete pieces of news using the admin page.

Your admin page should look like the following:

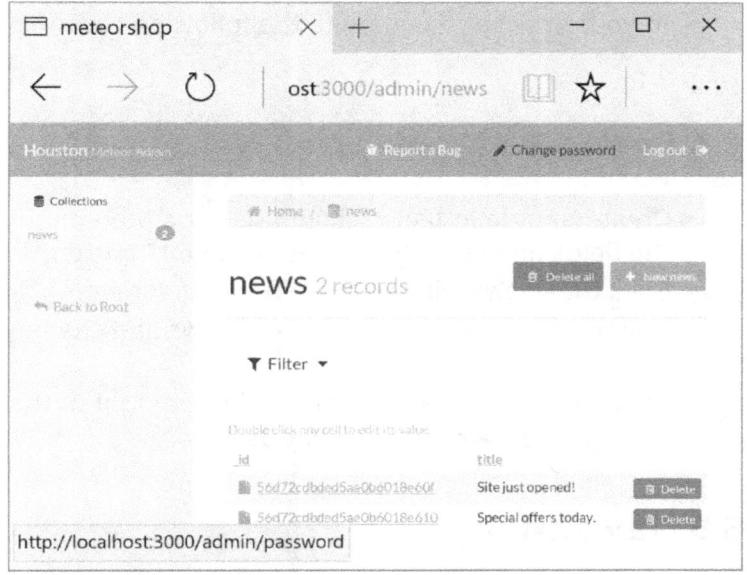

6.5 Exercise solution

- Leave your browser open and the meteor command-line running.
- Open another command-line, navigate to your application directory and type:

```
meteor add houston:admin
```

- Once the *"houston:admin: A zero-config Meteor Admin"* message is displayed, close the recently opened command-line.

- In your browser, navigate to the following URL:

```
http://localhost:3000/admin
```

- Create an admin user account as prompted: fill-in the fields and click the "Create account" button.
- Click the "news" link on the left of the screen.
- Double-click the title of a piece of news and change it.
- Click the "New news" button at the top right of the page, and create a piece of news.

6.6 Navigation

Chances are that your application is made of several pages. Those should be accessible through distinct URLs. Also, some data may be required on the client before displaying a page. For instance, you may want to make sure that a progress message is displayed before the home page while the news are being loaded.

Router packages are in charge of that. There are several router packages available for Meteor, one of which is *iron:router*. It allows for client or server-side routing.

To begin with, we of course need to add the package using the command line:

```
meteor add iron:router
```

Routes tell iron router what to display according to the incoming URL. They are described in a client and server JavaScript file, so for instance you can add them to a `routes.js` file in the root folder.

In its simplest form, you can render a template for a given route. In my previous examples I had templates named `messagesDisplay` and `messagesList`. Suppose I want `messagesList` to be displayed in the root page of my application and `messagesDisplay` to be available through the `http://localhost:3000/` message URL. I can write:

```
Router.route('/', function () {
  this.render('messagesList');
});

Router.route('/message', function () {
  this.render('messagesDisplay');
});
```

Now, we can either user HTML links or JavaScript to navigate to those URLs:

HTML navigation

```
<a href="/message">See one message</a>
```

JavaScript navigation

```
Router.go('/message');
```

Chances are that the messagesDisplay template will expect a parameter stating which message it should display. Routes can include parameters, and the render function can add data to the data context of the template. So for instance I could rewrite the /message route as such:

```
Router.route('/message/:id', function () {
  var id = this.params.id;
  this.render('messagesDisplay',
    { data: { id: id } }
  );
});
```

By default, the main application body will be displayed on each page. But you can provide a common layout as a template. Easy. Just create your layout as a template, then configure iron router to use it for all routes, or choose the layout in each route. And don't forget to remove the body (any HTML you have outside of template tags).

For instance, here are the layout and code to configure it for all pages. The layout should include a yield directive, which states where the page rendering should take place.

In any HTML file

```
<template name="mainLayout">
  <h1>My awesome application</h1>

  <div class="mainContent">
    {{> yield}}
  </div>

  <div class="footer">
    Copyright myself.
  </div>
</template>
```

routes.js

```
Router.configure({
  layoutTemplate: 'mainLayout'
});
```

More information about iron router is available in the iron router guide[2].

[2] http://iron-meteor.github.io/iron-router/

6.7 Exercise: Enable routing and create a layout

 Add the *iron:router* package to your application. Configure the following routes:

Path	Template
/	news
/time	time

Delete the `body` element and create a layout that contains a header with the following links:

Path	Title
/	Home
/time	Time

In the header, also add a link to the admin page you created earlier.

The home page should look like the following:

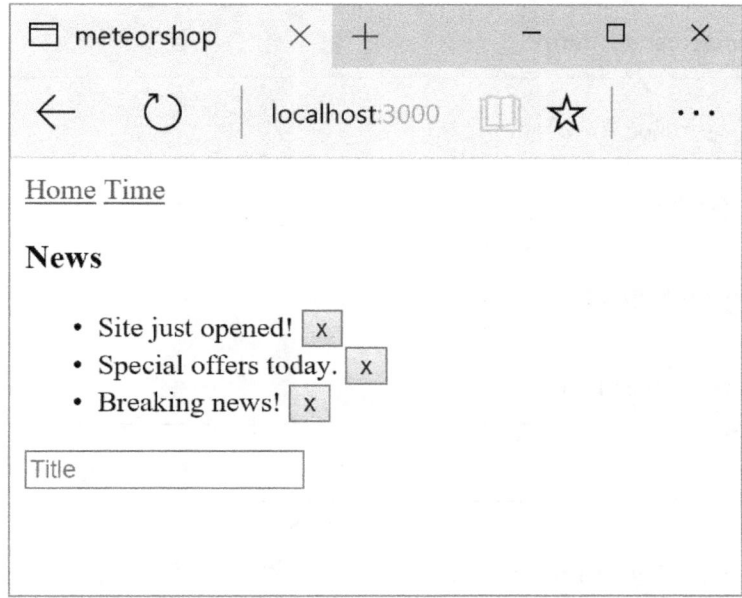

6.8 Exercise solution

- Point your browser to http://localhost:3000.
- Leave your browser open and the meteor command-line running.
- Open another command-line, navigate to your application directory and type:

```
meteor add iron:router
```

- Locate the following code:

Packages: admin dashboard, navigation, validation, forms generation

meteorshop.html

```
<body>
 <h1>Shop in a hurry</h1>
 ...
</body>
```

- Replace it with:

meteorshop.html

```
<body>
</body>
```

- Add a `layout.html` file in the `client` folder, with the following:

client/layout.html

```
<template name="layout">
 <div>
  <a href="/">Home</a>
  <a href="/time">Time</a>
  <a href="/time">Admin</a>
 </div>
 <div>
  {{>yield}}
 </div>
</template>
```

- Create a `routes.js` file in the root folder of your application and add the following code to it:

routes.js

```
Router.configure({
 layoutTemplate: 'layout'
});

Router.route('/', function () {
 this.render('news');
});

Router.route('/time', function () {
 this.render('timeDisplay');
});
```

- Switch back to your browser and try to navigate the application using the two links at the top.

6.9 Schemas, validation

Using Meteor, we are exposing a database to end users. Basic security concerns make it necessary to ensure that end users cannot compromise the system through their data input. For instance, as of now your application may be subject to script injection and several other hazards.

Furthermore, MongoDB is a schema-less database which makes it possible to add unstructured documents to its collections. While this may be a great productivity feature especially on rapidly evolving projects, it goes against security. For instance, our application relies on the fact that all news pieces contain a `title` field, so we should ensure that created and updated documents meet that condition.

Fortunately, there are two packages for that: *aldeed:simple-schema* and *aldeed:collection2*. The first, *aldeed:simple-schema*, allows us to create schemas for validating data. This feature can be used anywhere in the application, for instance for validating data which comes through a method parameter or a route. The example below shows how to check that some object has a `title` field of less than 100 characters, and that if the `price` field is a number (if present).

One-shot validation

```
var untrustedData = ...;

var schema = new SimpleSchema({
 title: {
  type: String,
  max: 200
 },
 price: {
  type: Number,
  optional: true
 }
});
```

```
var isValid = Match.test(untrustedData, schema);
```

Furthermore *aldeed:simple-schema* can be combined with other packages in order to make your work even easier. For instance when combined with the *aldeed:collection2* package, any update to a MongoDB collection is validated according to a schema. In other words, a schema is applied to your MongoDB collection. All you have to do is call the `attachSchema` method on a collection and provide it with a schema.

For intance, the following code will ensure that documents added or updated in the `Books` collection have a `title` field of less than 100 characters, and that if the `price` field is a number (if present):

MongoDB collection validation

```
var Schemas = {};

Schemas.Book = new SimpleSchema({
 title: {
  type: String,
  max: 200
 },
 price: {
  type: Number,
  optional: true
 }
});

Books.attachSchema(Schemas.Book);
```

Note that in the above example our schema is defined just as in the previous one-shot validation example. What's even greater is that those checks are made on the client and the server side, so a user is quickly notified **and** server data is safe.

6.10 Exercise: Create a collection and schema for the products

Your application is an e-store, so you need a way to store information about the products you sell.

Create a products collection. Create a schema for that collection using the *aldeed:simple-schema* package. The schema should enforce the following constraints:

- a title field must be present and be a String;
- a price field must be present and be a Number.

Make sure that whenever a document is added or modified in
the products collection, validation is applied using the schema you just created.

6.11 Exercise solution

- Leave your browser open and the `meteor` command-line running.
- Open another command-line, navigate to your application directory and type:

```
meteor add aldeed:simple-schema
meteor add aldeed:collection2
```

- Close that command-line once the packages were successfully installed.
- Add the following code at the top of the `meteorshop.js` file:

meteorshop.js

```
Products = new Mongo.Collection('products');

Products.attachSchema(new SimpleSchema({
 title: {
  type: String
 },
 price: {
  type: Number
 }
}));
```

6.12 CRUD forms generation

While coding a data-centric web application, a lot of time is spent creating forms. Forms allow users to create, update and delete data from your data store. But they require quite some work: create the UI, handle the events, perform validation and notify the user about any validation errors. That "quite some work" is multiplied by the number of collections, which in total amounts to an important part of the project.

Wouldn't it be nice to save a lot of time on that part? That's where another productive Meteor package kicks in: *aldeed:autoform*. This package will automatically create forms, complete with validation UI, and it can even connect them to your collections.

What's more, *aldeed:autoform* is very flexible. It can do anything from:

- Create a form connected to a MongoDB collection, including validation, all in just a line of code;
- Create a customized form connected to a MongoDB collection, including validation, with hooks you write;
- Create a UI that's validated using a schema you provide, calling your own functions when data is validated.

In other words, AutoForms can be coupled with collections or just schemas. Productivity **and** flexibility. Needless to say that this package should be part of most (if not all) of your projects.

In its most basic use, AutoForm is dead simple. Just reference your collection using the `quickForm` template. You need to provide a unique id. For instance, here is a form that allow users to add a new book:

```
{{> quickForm collection="Books" id="someId" type="in\
sert"}}
```

Your could change the `type` to `update`, and all you would need to do is provide the id of the document to be modified.

Should you need to customize the generated form, you can use the `autoForm` template in lieu of the `quickForm`. You can then specify the fields and customize the HTML content. And if you need insert, update and delete forms to be shown as popups, there are several packages that will do just that in a breeze.

AutoForm is really flexible, read more about it on the package page[3].

---

[3] https://github.com/aldeed/meteor-autoform

Packages: admin dashboard, navigation, validation, forms generation

6.13 Exercise: Create GUI for the user to display and add products with validation

Create a template named products that displays all documents in the products collection. For each product, display its title and price.

Make sure that users can navigate to the products template using the following URL: http//localhost:3000/products. Add a link to that URL in the header of your application, next to the other two links.

Add the *aldeed:autoform* package to your application. Add a form to the products template that allows users to add new products.

Your products page should look like the following:

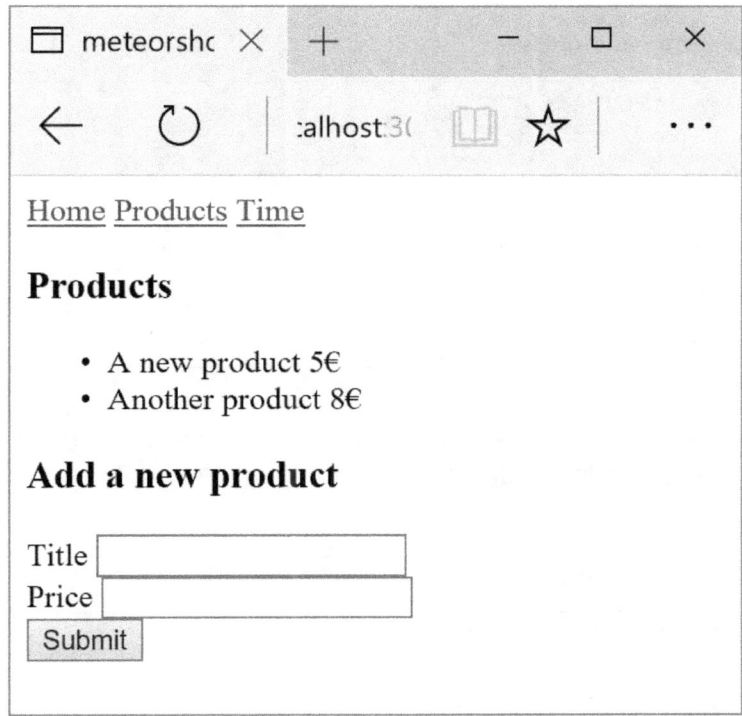

6.14 Exercise solution

- Leave your browser open and the meteor command-line running.
- Add a products.html file to the client folder. Add the following code:

client\products.html

```
<template name="products">
 <h3>Products</h3>
 <ul>
  {{#each list}}
  <li>{{title}} {{price}}$</li>
  {{/each}}
 </ul>
</template>
```

- Add a products.js file to the client folder. Add the following code:

client\products.js

```
Template.products.helpers({
 list: function () {
  return Products.find();
 }
});
```

- Open the route.js file. Add the following code after the one that is already in the file:

route.js

```js
Router.route('/products', function () {
 this.render('products');
});
```

- In the `client/layout.html` file, locate the following code:

client/layout.html

```html
...
<a href="/">Home</a>
<a href="/time">Time</a>
<a href="/admin">Admin</a>
...
```

- Replace that code with the following one :

client/layout.html

```html
...
<a href="/">Home</a>
<a href="/products">Products</a>
<a href="/time">Time</a>
<a href="/admin">Admin</a>
...
```

- Open another command-line, navigate to your application directory and type:

```
meteor add aldeed:autoform
```

- Once the package is added, close the recently opened command-line.
- In the `client/products.html` file, locate the following code:

client/products.html
```
...
</ul>
</template>
```

- Replace that code with the following one :

client/products.html
```
...
</ul>

<h3>Add a new product</h3>
{{> quickForm collection="Products" id="insertProduc\
tForm" type="insert"}}
</template>
```

- Switch back to your browser and click the "Products" link.
- Create some products using the form.
- Check that the products are being added.
- Try to create a product that has no price and no title. Check that a validation message appears and the product is not added.

6.15 Bootstrap

You surely know about Bootstrap, a widely used HTML framework using responsive design. Full use of Bootstrap goes beyond the scope of this book, but in case you don't know it you can get up to speed quickly by reading the documentation[4].

Although adding Bootstrap to an application is not a big deal, it's even easier using the Meteor package. Just type

```
meteor add twbs:bootstrap
```

Basically, Bootstrap relies on your pages having a root element with a `container` class. If your application uses some kind of layout (just like our exercises with `client/layout.html`) it's a no-brainer: add that element to the layout.

For instance, a layout using iron router would be:

```
<div class="container">
  {{>yield}}
</div>
```

You can also create a collapsable header (one that collapses on small screen sizes) using the `nav` element with a `navbar` class. Details and examples are available here in the Bootstrap documentation[5].

---

[4] http://getbootstrap.com/css/
[5] http://getbootstrap.com/components/#navbar

6.16 Exercise: Add some style to the application

> Styling your application is optional, and so is this exercise. If you don't want to spend time on styling your application, this is fine and you can skip this exercise altogether.

 Add Bootstrap to your application. Ensure that any page content is displayed in a `div` that has a CSS class of `container`.

Move the header links into a nav element that collapses.

Change the news page so that news are part of a Bootstrap list-group, and that the button to delete news has a beter style.

Your `news` page should now look like the following:

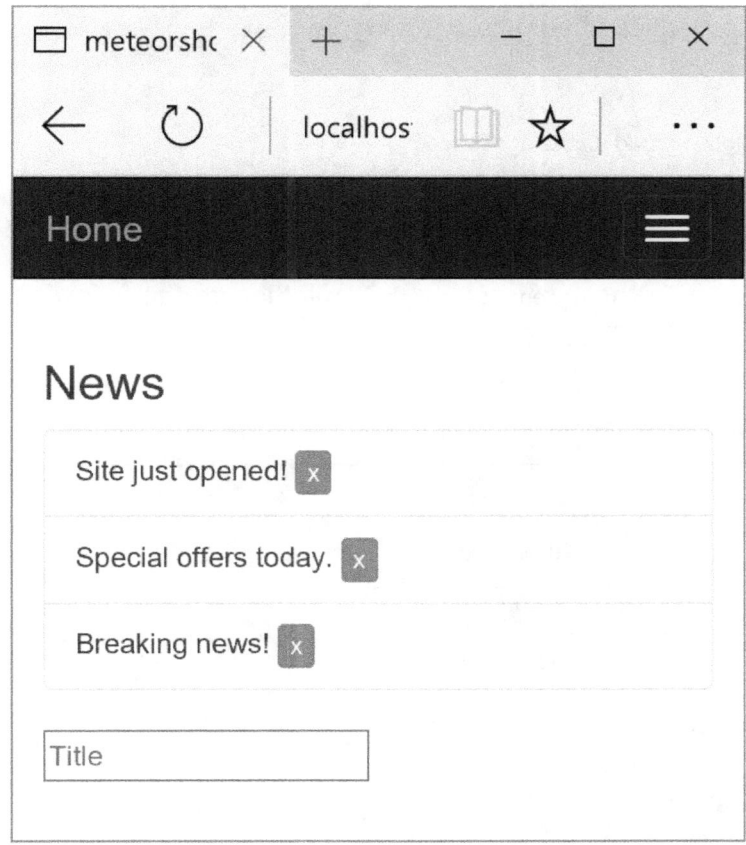

6.17 Exercise solution

- Leave your browser open and the meteor command-line running.
- Open another command-line, navigate to your ap-

Packages: admin dashboard, navigation, validation, forms generation

plication directory and type:

```
meteor add twbs:bootstrap
```

- Once the package is added, close the recently opened command-line.
- In the `client/layout.html` file, locate the following code:

client/layout.html

```
<template name="layout">
 <div>
  <a href="/">Home</a>
  <a href="/products">Products</a>
  <a href="/time">Time</a>
  <a href="/admin">Admin</a>
 </div>
 <div>
  {{>yield}}
 </div>
</template>
```

- Replace that code with the following one :

client/layout.html

```html
<template name="layout">
 <nav class="navbar navbar-inverse">
  <div class="container-fluid">
   <div class="navbar-header">
    <button type="button"
      class="navbar-toggle collapsed"
      data-toggle="collapse"
      data-target="#nvbc1"
      aria-expanded="false">
     <span class="icon-bar"></span>
     <span class="icon-bar"></span>
     <span class="icon-bar"></span>
    </button>
    <a class="navbar-brand" href="/">Home</a>
   </div>
   <div class="collapse navbar-collapse" id="nvbc1">
    <ul class="nav navbar-nav">
     <li><a href="/products">Products</a></li>
     <li><a href="/time">Time</a></li>
     <li><a href="/admin">Admin</a></li>
    </ul>
   </div>
  </div>
 </nav>
 <div class="container">
  {{>yield}}
 </div>
</template>
```

Packages: admin dashboard, navigation, validation, forms generation

- In the `client/news.html` file, locate the following code:

client/news.html

```
...
<ul>
 {{#each news}}
   <li>{{title}} <button class="removeAction">x</butto\
n></li>
 {{/each}}
</ul>
...
```

- Replace that code with the following one :

client/news.html

```
...
<ul class="list-group">
 {{#each news}}
   <li class="list-group-item">
     {{title}}
     <button class="btn btn-danger btn-xs removeAction"\
>x</button>
   </li>
 {{/each}}
</ul>
...
```

- Switch back to your browser and click the "Home" link.
- Check the new style.
- Resize the browser window so that its width gets smaller and wider. The navigation bar should collapse on smaller widths.

7. Accounts: user management

7.1 Meteor's account system

Meteor relies on packages for user management. Several packages are provided by the Meteor team, plus many third-parties packages.

At the root of user management is the *accounts-base* package, which provides a `Meteor.users` collection and an API. Full access to the collection is restricted to server-side code for obvious security reasons, and the client-side code has access to a restricted API enabling you to check whether the user is authenticated: `Meteor.user()`. It returns `null` when the user isn't authenticated, otherwise you get some of the user details (a subset of the fields available on the server).

> Since several account-related packages rely on the *accounts-base* package and add it automatically, there is usually no need to add it from the command line.

Sure, you could code everything manually starting from *accounts-base*. But remember: Meteor is about productivity. So they provide lots of packages to get you going.

Basically, what we need is a way to authenticate users and a UI for doing so. For the first part, you simply add a login provider package. For the second part, you have the choice between a ready-to-use UI package or extended packages that let you customize the appearance. Let's see about those two parts.

Login providers

Users may authenticate against your database, a third-party, or whatever you may come up with like two-steps authentication or token-based one-time passwords. There are many packages available for that, like:

- *accounts-password*: password-based login;
- *accounts-facebook*, *accounts-google*, *accounts-twitter* and several others: third-party authentication using OAuth;
- many others, just look for them in Atmosphere[1].

Login UI packages

There are two ways to create your authentication UI:

The super-fast one, great for prototyping: add the *accounts-ui* package, use the `{{> loginButtons}}` template

---

[1] https://atmospherejs.com/?q=accounts-

to get login buttons and you're done. Downside is: you cannot customize the look of the generated UI.

The fully customizable one, which takes slightly more time, where you use one of the packages based on *useraccounts*. For instance, you may use *useraccounts:bootstrap*, *useraccounts:materialize* or *useraccounts:polymer* that are ready made for the popular frameworks, or *useraccounts:unstyled* in case you need custom HTML.

Using any of the packages based on *useraccounts*, all you need to do is include the `{{> atForm}}` template. It will adapt to whatever login state the user is in in order to create a login or register form. Also, you can use the `{{> atNavButton}}` template that will create a "Log-in" / "Log-out" button.

The full list of *useraccounts* UI packages can be found here[2].

Restricting access to parts the application

Once your users are authenticated, you'll surely need to have pages restricted to authenticated users or groups. For that purpose, The *useraccounts:iron-routing* can be combined with the *iron:router* package we used earlier.

In fact, *useraccounts:iron-routing* is simple to use, yet configurable. You only have two things to do. First you state which layout should be used:

---

[2] https://github.com/meteor-useraccounts/core/blob/master/Guide.md

```
AccountsTemplates.configure({
  defaultLayout: 'layout',
});
```

In fact, the `AccountsTemplates.configure` function allows you to configure all of the behavior of the *useraccounts:<whatever>* packages and you can see the whole list of options here[3].

Next, you can use the `Router.plugin` method in order to state which pages should be accessible only to authenticated users. That method will accept `only` and `except` options which are arrays of routes (as strings).

For instance, here is how we would restrict access to the `prices` and `admin` routes to authenticated users:

```
Router.plugin('ensureSignedIn', {
    only: ['prices', 'admin']
});
```

---

[3] https://github.com/meteor-useraccounts/core/blob/master/Guide.md

7.2 Exercise: Secure the products management

 You must enable an authentication system using a login and password on your application.

Only authenticated users should be able to access the Products page. Unauthenticated users should be redirected to a login page when trying to access the Products page.

In the header of the application, add a "Log-in" / "Log-out" button.

Here is what an unauthenticated user should see when clicking on the *Products* link:

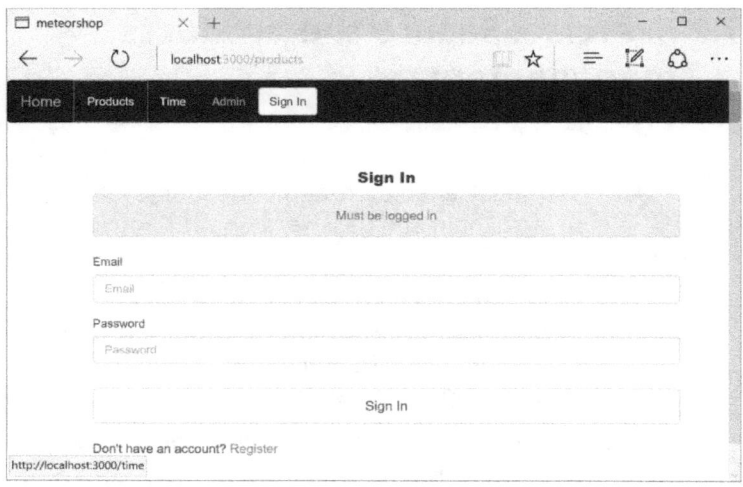

7.3 Exercise solution

- Point your browser to http://localhost:3000.
- Leave your browser open and the meteor command-line running.
- Open another command-line, navigate to your application directory and type:

```
meteor add accounts-password
meteor add useraccounts:bootstrap
meteor add useraccounts:iron-routing
```

- Add the following code to the end of the route.js file:

route.js

```
AccountsTemplates.configure({
 defaultLayout: 'layout',
});

Router.plugin('ensureSignedIn', {
 only: ['products']
});
```

- Locate the following code:

client/layout.html

```
  <li><a href="/admin">Admin</a></li>
</ul>
```

- Replace it with:

client/layout.html

```
  <li><a href="/admin">Admin</a></li>
  <li>{{> atNavButton}}</li>
</ul>
```

- Switch back to your browser and try to navigate the application using the two links at the top. Note that the *Products* page cannot be accessed if you are not logged-in.

- Create an account using the link at the bottom of the login page, and check that you can access the whole application.
- Logout, check that the *Products* page cannot be accessed anymore.
- Log-in and check that you can access the whole application.

8. Going further

8.1 MiniMongo: you don't even need MongoDB

As we saw earlier, `Mongo.Collection` allows you to have real-time, synchronized, client **and** server access to MongoDB collections. This is great, but what if you need a simple in-memory store for data? Well, you can, and you already know how.

When you create a `Mongo.Collection`, it uses MiniMongo on the client side in order to cache query results. The good news is that you can create a MiniMongo instance alone. Just create a new `Mongo.Collection` using `null` as the constructor parameter (instead of the MongoDB collection name that you would provide otherwise) and you get an in-memory MiniMongo. What's more, this MiniMongo isn't synchronized between the server and client like a normal `Mongo.Collection`: it remains only where you declared it: server-side when declared on the server and, well, client-side if declared on the client.

To summarize, just write:

```
var store = new Meteor.Collection(null);
```

And that's all. You can now query that collection using the `find` method, and update it using update methods (almost) just like a MongoDB collection.

MiniMongo is a reactive collection, which means that pages displaying data from a MiniMongo collection will get instantly updated when the data held in MiniMongo changes.

Using client-only or server-only in-memory MiniMongo comes in handy for parts of your application where you store temporary data. For persistent data, use the full power of Mongo-stored collections. That is, create a `Mongo.Collection` providing the MongoDB collection name as a string parameter.

8.2 Exercise: Create and manage a shopping cart

Display the list of products on the home page. Next to each product in the list, add a "Buy" button.

Create an in-memory collection that holds items in the shopping cart. When the user clicks the "Buy" button, add a new item to the shopping cart, with a quantity of 1.

Add a "Cart" page and link to it from the header.

On the "Cart" page, display a list of items in the cart together with the quantity. Next to each cart item, add "+" and "-" buttons that increase or decrease the quantity.

Here is what the "Cart" page should look like:

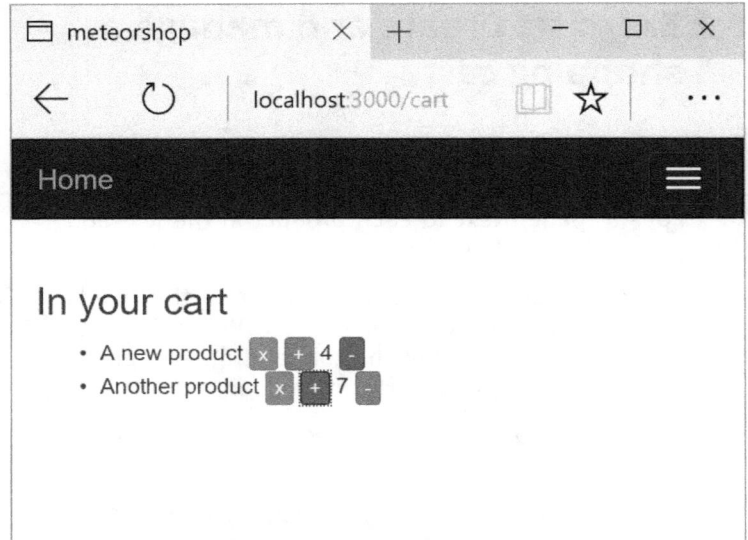

8.3 Exercise solution

- Point your browser to `http://localhost:3000`.
- Leave your browser open and the `meteor` command-line running.
- Add a `store.html` file in the `client` folder, with the following code:

client/store.html

```
<template name="store">
 <h3>Store</h3>
 <ul>
  {{#each list}}
  <li>
   {{title}} {{price}}$
   <button class="btn btn-success btn-xs buyAction">
    Buy
   </button>
  </li>
  {{/each}}
 </ul>
</template>
```

- Add a `store.js` file in the `client` folder, with the following code:

client/store.js

```
Basket = new Mongo.Collection(null);

Template.store.helpers({
 list: function () {
  return Products.find();
 }
});

Template.store.events({
```

```
  'click .buyAction': function () {
    Basket.insert({ product: this, quantity: 1});
  }
});
```

- Add a home.html file in the client folder, with the following:

client/home.html
```
<template name="home">
 <div class="row">
  <div class="col-sm-7">
   {{> store}}
  </div>
  <div class="col-sm-5">
   {{> news}}
  </div>
 </div>
</template>
```

> In the template above, the div elements are there in order to have side-by-side columns using Bootstrap CSS classes. We could as well have avoided them since they don't change the functionality.

- Locate the following code:

route.js

```
Router.route('/', function () {
 this.render('news');
});
```

- **Replace it with:**

route.js

```
Router.route('/', function () {
 this.render('home');
});

Router.route('/cart', function () {
 this.render('cart');
});
```

- **Locate the following code:**

client/layout.html

```
...
<li><a href="/products">Products</a></li>
...
```

- **Replace it with:**

client/layout.html

```
...
<li><a href="/products">Products</a></li>
<li><a href="/cart">Cart</a></li>
...
```

- **Add a** cart.html **file in the** client **folder, with the following:**

client/cart.html

```
<template name="cart">
 <h3>In your cart</h3>
 <ul>
  {{#each contents}}
  <li>{{product.title}}
   <button
   class="removeAction btn btn-xs btn-danger">
    x
   </button>
   <button
   class="incrementAction btn btn-xs btn-primary">
    +
   </button>
   {{quantity}}
   <button
   class="decrementAction btn btn-xs btn-primary">
    -
   </button>
```

```
    </li>
    {{/each}}
  </ul>
</template>
```

- Add a `cart.js` file in the `client` folder, with the following:

client/cart.js

```
Template.cart.helpers({
    contents: function () {
        return Basket.find();
    }
});

Template.cart.events({
  'click .removeAction': function() {
    Basket.remove({_id: this._id});
  },
  'click .incrementAction': function() {
    Basket.update({_id: this._id},
    {$inc: {quantity: 1}});
  },
  'click .decrementAction': function() {
    Basket.update({
      _id: this._id,
      quantity: { $gt: 1 },
    },
    {$inc: {quantity: -1 }});
```

```
    }
});
```

> In the code above, `quantity: { $gt: 1 }` is a condition that checks that the quantity is 1 or more before decrementing. This way we ensure there can't be negative quantities.

- Switch back to your browser.
- Navigate to the home page. Check that it displays a list of products.
- Add some products to your cart using the "Buy" button next to the products.
- Navigate to the "Cart" page. Check that the products you added to your cart appear there.
- Try to increment and decrement the number of products in your cart.

8.4 Getting out of prototyping

Up to now we've been coding our application really fast, which is great for prototyping. However, for our coding to be so effective Meteor uses two packages that should be removed before going to production, since they compromise security:

- The *autopublish* package, which ensures that all the collections you declared using `Mongo.Collection` are available to the client;
- The *insecure* package, which allows the client to make any change to the collections.

The *autopublish* package lowers security since it enables any client to get all of the documents in each collection.

The *insecure* package lowers security because, even though your GUI allows only for certain changes, an evil developer could execute custom JavaScript code on the client that would make unexpected changes to your collections.

Thus, you obviously want to remove the *autopublish* and *insecure* package before moving your application to production. Let's see how.

Removing *autopublish*

First, you need to remove the package. Just run the following command on your command line:

```
meteor remove autopublish
```

Now, you need to tell Meteor which data should be published and fetched. This is done in two steps:

1. Use the `Meteor.publish` function on the server;
2. Call the `Meteor.subscribe` function on the client.

For both functions, you provide a publication name as a string, that should be the same on the client and server (that's how the subscription is matched with the publication). You can also take parameters in the publish method, that you provide in the subscribe method.

To keep things simple, a subscribe should be done before you fetch documents from a collection on the client, for instance before using the collection `find` method. A good place to do so is in the onCreated event of a template where you use the data.

Let's have a look at an example. Remember the code I used in order to display all the books:

demos.js

```
Books = new Meteor.Collection('books');

if (Meteor.isClient) {
  Template.books.helpers({
    books: function () {
      return Books.find({});
    }
  });
}
```

demos.html

```
<template name="books">
    <ul>
        {{#each book in books}}
        <li>{{book.title}}</li>
        {{/each}}
    </ul>
</template>
```

This code was based on the *autopublish* package being present. It won't work anymore once the *autopublish* package is removed. Let's fix this. First, I have to publish the data used by that template. I'll choose a name of `books-all` for this subscription. In a `server/publications.js` file I write:

server/publications.js

```
Meteor.publish("books-all", function () {
  return Books.find({});
});
```

Next, I subscribe to that publication in the `onCreated` event of the `books` template. I create a `client/books.js` file and add the following code:

client/books.js

```
Template.books.onCreated(function() {
 this.subscribe('books-all');
});
```

Now, after those two steps the list of books is displayed again.

Note that I use `this.subscribe` instead of `Meteor.subscribe`. This allows for the subscription to be gracefully disposed of when the template is not being displayed.

When using *iron:router*, you can have the router render a waiting template while the subscription gets effectively available on the client. For this, you provide a `waitOn` option that gets a subscription or array of subscriptions:

```
Router.route('/books', {
  loadingTemplate: 'loading',

  waitOn: function () {
    return Meteor.subscribe('books-all');
  },

  action: function () {
   this.render('books');
  }
});
```

8.5 Exercise: Remove the *autopublish* package

 Remove the *autopublish* package in order to make the application more secure. Note that the application pages do not display data anymore.

Make sure to add the appropriate calls to *publish* and *subscribe* methods in order to display the data.

8.6 Exercise solution

- Point your browser to `http://localhost:3000`.
- Leave your browser open and the `meteor` command-line running.
- Open another command-line, navigate to your application directory and type:

```
meteor remove autopublish
```

- Switch back to your browser and note that news and products are not displayed anymore on the home page and *Products* page.
- Create a `server/publications.js` file with the following code:

server/publications.js

```
Meteor.publish("news-all", function () {
 return News.find();
});
Meteor.publish("products-all", function () {
 return Products.find();
});
```

- Create a `client/subscriptions.js` file with the following code:

server/subscriptions.js

```
Template.news.onCreated(function() {
 this.subscribe('news-all');
});
Template.products.onCreated(function() {
 this.subscribe('products-all');
});
Template.store.onCreated(function() {
 this.subscribe('products-all');
});
```

- Switch back to your browser and note that news and products are displayed again on the home page and *Products* page.

Removing *insecure*

First, you need to remove the package. Just run the following command on your command line:

```
meteor remove insecure
```

When you do so, a client can only perform limited update operations on the collections. For instance, it can update a document providing its _id field but it cannot remove documents or insert new ones. If you decided that the client code should not even be able to update a document providing its _id field, you can use the `deny` option when creating a `Meteor.Collection`.

Now, only server code has access to the full range update operations. Since your client code needs to make updates too, you can enable them using methods. Methods are declared on the client **and** server (common code) with a name and parameters, and called from the client using the same name.

> Methods are more powerful than a basic API call. When a method is called on the client, it is first evaluated on the client using the data that's already cached by MiniMongo. That way, a user sees immediate results to their action. Then the method is evaluated on the server, and any change is pushed to the client so the user sees the real result taking into account full server-side data.

Here is how you declare methods:

commoncode.js

```
Meteor.methods({
  'deletebook': function(id) {
    Books.remove({_id: id});
  },
  'dosomething': function(first, second) {
    ...
  }
});
```

And here is how you would call those methods from client-side events:

```
Template.books.events({
  'click .deleteAction': function(e, a) {
    Meteor.call('deletebook', this._id);
  },
  'click .doAction': function(e, a) {
    var first = ...;
    var seconcd = ...;
    Meteor.call('dosomething', first, second);
  }
});
```

8.7 Exercise: Remove the *insecure* package

Remove the *insecure* package in order to make the application more secure. Check that you cannot add or remove news pieces using the home page anymore.

Make sure to add the appropriate calls to *methods* and *call* methods in order to enable users to add or remove news pieces using the home page.

8.8 Exercise solution

- Point your browser to `http://localhost:3000`.
- Leave your browser open and the `meteor` command-line running.
- Open another command-line, navigate to your application directory and type:

```
meteor remove insecure
```

- Switch back to your browser and note that you cannot add or remove news pieces on the home page.
- Create a `methods.js` file with the following code:

methods.js

```
Meteor.methods({
  'removenews': function(id) {
    News.remove({_id: id});
  },
  'insertnews': function(title) {
    News.insert({
      title: title,
      created: new Date()
    });
  }
});
```

- Locate the following code:

client/client.js

```
Template.news.events({
  'submit form': function (e) {
    e.preventDefault();
    var title = e.target.title.value;
    News.insert({title: title, created: new Date()});
  },
  'click .removeAction': function(e, a) {
    News.remove({_id: this._id});
  }
});
```

- Replace it with:

client/client.js

```
Template.news.events({
 'submit form': function (e) {
  e.preventDefault();
  var title = e.target.title.value;
  Meteor.call('insertnews', title);
 },
 'click .removeAction': function(e, a) {
  Meteor.call('removenews', this._id);
 }
});
```

> Note that direct calls to collections methods were replaced with method calls.

- Switch back to your browser and note that you can now add or remove news pieces on the home page.

Definitions

Bundling

Bundling is the process of combining in a single file several JavaScript or CSS files. Since a browser is limited in the amount of files it can get at at time from the server, and since each HTTP request has overhead, bundling enables for faster load times on the client.

Bundling is often done together with minification.

Minification

The process of reducing the size of CSS and JavaScript files without altering their meaning. This can be done by removing extra spaces and renaming local variables to shorter names.

Minification is done on the server during the build process, so that the files provided to the client are smaller. That way, they get to the client quicker, which means faster load times.

Minification is often done together with bundling.

npm

npm is a popular JavaScript package manager. Basically, a package manager allows you to download a library into your application folder so you can use it. Why not simply download it manually? Well, npm will also manage dependencies (packages needed by that particular package) and download them if needed. It will also allow you to manage versions and update packages painlessly.

Spacebars

Spacebars is the default syntax used to write Meteor templates. It is derived from the Handlebars[1] syntax.

Spacebars is HTML with extensions. Extensions take the form of mustache tags like the following:

```
{{#each product in products}}
<li>Buy {{product.name}} now!</li>
{{/each}}
```

---

[1] http://handlebarsjs.com

A word from the author

I sincerely hope you enjoyed reading this book as much as I liked writing it and that you quickly become proficient enough with Meteor.

If you would like to get in touch you can use :

- email: books@aweil.fr
- Facebook: https://facebook.com/learncollection

In case your project needs it, I'm also available for speaking, teaching, consulting and coding. All around the world.

If you liked this book, you probably saved a lot of time thanks to it. I'd be very grateful if you took some minutes of your precious time to leave a comment on the site where you purchased this book. Thanks a ton !

The Learn collection

This book is part of the *Learn collection*.

The *Learn collection* allows developers to self-teach new technologies in a matter of days.

Published books

- Learn ASP.NET MVC[2]
- Learn Meteor[3]

To be published in 2016

- Learn Knockout
- Learn WPF

---

[2] http://tinyurl.com/h6hjwce
[3] https://leanpub.com/learnmeteor

www.ingramcontent.com/pod-product-compliance
Lightning Source LLC
Chambersburg PA
CBHW060859170526
45158CB00001B/418